Our WILD™
WORLD
SERIES

Bats

NorthWord
Minnetonka, Minnesota

DEDICATION
To Eli, who helped me every day in (almost) every way.
–J.V.

ACKNOWLEDGEMENTS:
Many thanks to Rob Mies and Kim Williams, researchers, educators, and conservationists
at the Organization for Bat Conservation, for sharing their expertise.

Photography © 2007: All photos provided by Merlin D. Tuttle, Bat Conservation International except for the following: Christian
Ziegler/Minden Pictures: p. 4; Martin Withers/FLPA/Minden Pictures: p. 7; Shutterstock: pp. 10, 30; Michael Durham/Minden
Pictures: p. 19; Hugo Willocx/Foto Natura/Minden Pictures: pp. 20, 45; Stephen Dalton/Minden Pictures: pp. 24-25; Karen Marks,
Bat Conservation International: pp. 28-29; Joe McDonald/Bruce Coleman: p. 40; Michael & Patricia Fogden/Minden Pictures: p. 41.

Illustrations by Andrew Recher
Designed by Laurie Fritsche
Edited by Kristen McCurry
Front cover image: Gambian epauletted fruit bats
Back cover image: Eastern pipistrelle bat

NorthWord Books for Young Readers
11571 K-Tel Drive
Minnetonka, MN 55343
1-888-255-9989
www.tnkidsbooks.com

Library of Congress Cataloging-in-Publication Data

Vogel, Julia
        Bats / by Julia Vogel ; illustrations by Andrew Recher.
                p. cm. – (Our wild world series)
        ISBN-13: 978-1-55971-968-1 (hardcover) – ISBN-13: 978-1-55971-969-8 (softcover)
        1. Bats—Juvenile literature. I. Recher, Andrew, ill. II. Title.

QL737.C5V64 2007
599.4--dc22

                                                    2006021917

Printed in Singapore

10 9 8 7 6 5 4 3 2 1

Our **WILD**™
WORLD
SERIES

Bats

Julia Vogel
Illustrations by Andrew Recher

NORTHWORD
Minnetonka, Minnesota

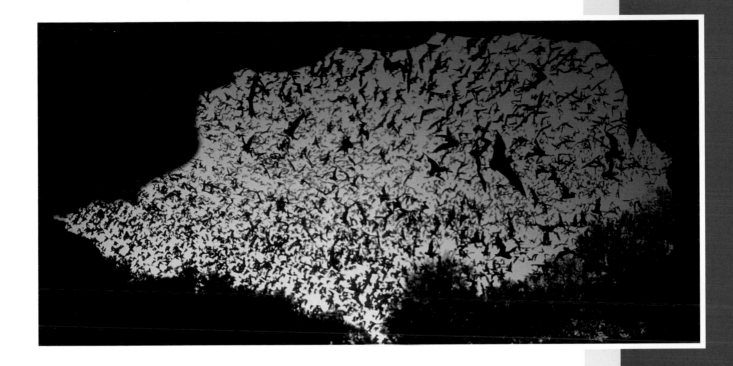

JUST BEFORE SUNSET, dark shapes begin to dart out of Bracken Cave in the Texas hill country. First one, then three, then 10, then hundreds and thousands of Mexican free-tailed bats spiral into the evening sky. It can take over two hours for all 20 million bats to leave their daytime shelter, or roost, for another night of hunting insects.

The sight of the world's largest bat colony would fill many people with dread. Storytellers through history have spun tales of bats as mysterious nightmare creatures, friends of ghouls and witches, and evil messengers of a dark underworld. Many people shudder at just the mention of the word "bat."

Yet each summer, more people visit Bracken Cave to watch the bats. They are learning that bats are not dangerous, and that they are fascinating animals with unique traits and surprising abilities unlike those of any other wildlife. People who know a little about these night fliers cannot wait to learn more about bats.

By day, most bats rest in shelters such as caves and hollow trees for protection against bad weather and natural enemies.

In one night, millions of bats from Bracken Cave can eat 200 tons of moths and other insects.

Like dogs, mice, and humans, bats are mammals, which are warm-blooded animals that have fur (hair) and nurse their young. But unlike any other mammals, bats can fly. So-called flying lemurs and flying squirrels can only glide on the wind from one perch to another. In contrast, bats have chest and back muscles that power their wings during flights as high as 10,000 feet (3,050 m) and as fast as 60 miles (97 km) per hour. Because bats are so unusual, scientists place them in their own order, or group, called *Chiroptera* (ky-ROP-ter-uh). The name means "hand-wing" in Greek.

Worldwide, there are over 1,000 kinds, or species (SPEE-sees), of bats. About 200 species are grouped together as *Megachiroptera*, or megabats. Often called "flying foxes" for their fox-like faces, megabats live only in tropical parts of Africa, Asia, and Australia. The rest of the world's bats,

Bats
FUNFACT:

In China, bats are symbols of good luck.
The Chinese character *wu-fu* shows five bats
with wings touching, representing health,
wealth, long life, good luck, and happiness.

Some of the biggest bats in the world live in Australia. Sometimes so many spectacled flying foxes roost in the same tree that limbs break off from the weight.

the *Microchiroptera*, live on every continent except Antarctica. With over 800 species, these microbats live in many different habitats, including forests, deserts, grasslands, cities, and suburbs. All 47 species of bats native to the United States and Canada are microbats.

Usually, megabats are larger than microbats. One of the largest bat species is the Malayan flying fox, which can weigh 2.5 pounds (1.1 kg) and measure 6 feet (1.8 m) from wingtip to wingtip. The tiniest species is a microbat found in Thailand's rain forests, called the bumblebee bat. Weighing less than 0.07 ounce (2 g)— about the same as a dime—it's the world's smallest mammal.

Honduran white bats roost under tents they make from leaves of bananas and other rain forest plants.

Bats also sport a variety of fur coats. Some have short, velvety fur, while others are fluffy, like Persian cats. A few have thick, soft fur collars around their necks. Most are dark in color, often brown, gray, or black, without bold markings. Within one species, individuals may vary in color. North America's little brown bats range from light tan to deep brown, and southeastern bats may be brown or gray. These plain colors camouflage (KAM-uh-flaj) the bats, helping them to hide from their enemies while they rest in trees or other roosts.

Unexpected colors and patterns appear on many species, though. Honduran white bats have pure white body fur with yellow noses and ears. Pallid bats are usually cream-colored, and silver-haired bats have jet black fur tipped with a frosting of white. In eastern red bats, one of the few species where males and females may differ in color, females may be reddish brown and males bright orange. A few species have striking patterns. Spectacled (SPEK-tuh-kuld) bats look like they are wearing glasses, and epauletted (eh-puh-LET-ed) fruit bats have white shoulder patches that males flash at females during courtship. One bat has almost no fur at all, the naked bat of Borneo and the Philippines.

Eastern red bats often roost alone in North American forests. Dangling from a branch by one foot, they hide from enemies by looking like dead leaves.

Horseshoe bats get their name from horseshoe-shaped flesh surrounding their nostrils. Unlike many other bats, horseshoe bats echolocate through their noses.

Bats also have other traits that help you tell one species from another. Fox-faced megabats usually have big eyes, long noses, and large, pointed ears. Microbats have small eyes, but their ears and noses come in amazing varieties. As examples, the short, rounded ears on yellow bats look elf-like, while some big-eared bats' ears look long enough for a rabbit.

The names of many bats give clues to their nose shapes. There are tube-nosed bats, hog-nosed bats, leaf-nosed bats, and sword-nosed bats. Each special nose shape helps the bat survive. In Arizona, for example, lesser long-nosed bats have just the right nose shape to poke into a saguaro (su-WAHR-oh) cactus blossom for their favorite food, sugary cactus nectar.

Of course, all bats have wings. Roosting bats wrap their wings tightly around their bodies for warmth on cold nights or fan their wings in hot weather to cool off. Mother bats hug their babies with their wings while roosting. During flight, a wing can scoop up a moth and sweep it into the bat's mouth.

Bats
FUNFACT:

Big brown bats and several other species will roost in bat houses. They can be picky about the kind of house they use, so scientists are experimenting to learn what house size, shape, and location bats like best.

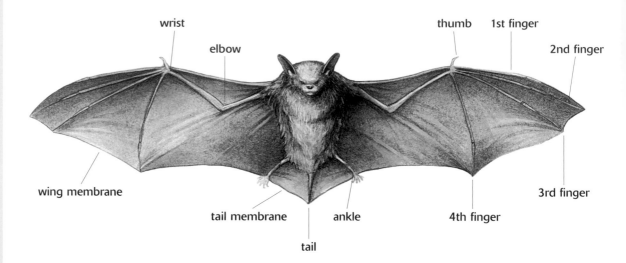

wrist elbow thumb 1st finger 2nd finger wing membrane tail membrane ankle 4th finger 3rd finger tail

Unlike feathery bird wings, bat wings are two layers of tough, thin skin stretched over arm and hand bones. Each wing's lower edge attaches to the bat's ankle. In most bats, another membrane stretches between the hind legs and tail. Hundreds of tiny muscles between the skin layers gather the wings up, like a closed accordion, for protection when not needed. Wing injuries heal quickly, but a large tear can mean doom for the bat.

Bats do not flap their wings up and down to fly. Instead, they fly as if they are swimming the butterfly stroke. Four extra-long, slim finger bones support each wing membrane and can move as freely as our fingers, easily changing the wing's shape and position. This ability allows bats to turn, dive, and flip, making them more acrobatic than birds.

How do bats find food and avoid crashes with trees or each other at night? Bats are not blind, as many people believe. A microbat's small eyes probably cannot see colors, but they can see better than human eyes can in the dark. Megabats' large eyes are even more sensitive to light, plus they can see colors. With their keen eyesight, flying foxes easily spot fruiting or flowering plants in the dim light of dusk or dawn.

Smells of fruit and flowers also attract bats. Plants such as organ-pipe cacti open their blossoms only at night, and the sweet perfume draws nectar-eating bats from near and far. A fruit bat can follow its nose to a fig tree, then sniff each fig to pick the ripest ones. Insect-eating bats also have a keen sense of smell, and many species of both megabats and microbats have scent glands on their faces and wings that produce odors. Bats use these smells to recognize each other and sometimes to attract mates.

Bats
FUNFACT:

A bat roost in Austin, Texas, has become a major tourist attraction. On summer nights, hundreds of tourists join many locals to watch thousands of Mexican free-tailed bats leave the Congress Avenue Bridge for a night of hunting.

Hearing, though, may be a bat's most important sense. A bat's ears can be more than twice as large as the rest of its head. Even small bat ears can turn and tilt to catch more sounds, and many bat ears have special shapes, folds, wrinkles, or skin flaps to improve their sound-collecting ability. A pallid bat's tall ears twist and turn as it flies close to the ground, listening for crickets, centipedes, or other prey. It will land ready to pounce if it hears the tiny taps of a scorpion's feet in the desert sand.

Unlike other North American bats, pallid bats hunt for scorpions and other prey on the ground and carry them to rocky perches to eat later.

Bats make plenty of sounds themselves. Roosts often echo with squeaks and squeals of chatting bats. In a crowded attic, one bat may squawk to warn another out of its space, or a mother and baby may chirp back and forth to find each other in the crowd.

Africa's hammer-headed bats can call as loud as car alarms, and 100 males may gather in mating season to clang and croak for females. The deafening choruses have earned the animals the nickname "noise boxes with wings."

The most amazing sounds that bats make are the key to flying swiftly in total darkness. In 1938, zoologist (zo-OL-uh-jist) Donald Griffin used a newly-invented microphone to discover that bats make ultrasonic (ul-tra-SAWN-ik) calls: clicks and squeaks too high for human ears to detect. The ultrasonic cries are part of a complex system that sends out sound waves to bounce off nearby objects and echo back to the bat's ears. A sound picture develops in the bat's brain that allows it to find and catch tasty snacks and avoid slamming into walls. Only bats, dolphins, some whales, and a few other kinds of animals have this remarkable ability, which Dr. Griffin named echolocation (ek-oh-lo-KAY-shun). A bat's echolocation system works better than any sonar yet invented by humans.

Bats
FUNFACT:

Bat echolocation can detect objects as thin as a human hair, yet researchers can catch bats when they fly into nets. Why? Scientists think that bats get used to flying safely along certain paths and sometimes do not notice new obstacles in their way.

All microbats, including all bats living in North America, can echolocate. An echolocating microbat produces sounds by vibrating chords in its larynx (LAIR-inks), or voice box. Some bats, such as leaf-nosed bats, send the beeps and other calls out their noses. The odd-looking nose flaps on these bats are believed to help direct the sounds toward their targets. Most bats, though, send ultrasonic blasts out of their mouths. A bat flying with its mouth open, sharp teeth bared, may look fierce, but it is really echolocating.

At first, a hunting little brown bat sends out calls fairly slowly, perhaps 10 chirps per second. But when the echoes show prey ahead, clicking may speed up to 200 per second. The faster "feeding buzz" gives the bat a clearer picture of what it is chasing, which way the prey is going, and how fast the insect is moving. It hurries to snag the bug in its mouth, wing, or tail membrane and swallow it fast. After all, it cannot call again if its mouth is full.

Bats
FUNFACT:

Some insects have developed the ability to detect echolocation signals from bats. When some moths hear ultrasonic bat clicks, they fly in loops or dive to avoid capture.

If we could hear the high pitch of a little brown bat, it would be as loud as a fire alarm.

Each bat species echolocates in its own way, and individuals also vary the type, frequency, and loudness of their calls. "Whispering bats," for example, call softly as they search for bugs hiding among plant leaves, while "shouting bats" blast sound at insects in the open air above lakes, clearings, and backyards. Scientists study echolocation differences using a device called a bat detector. Detectors change ultrasonic bat bleeps into sounds people can hear, so we can eavesdrop on bats as they hunt under the stars.

Though they roost in dark caves and rock crevices, Egyptian fruit bats feed in open forests on fruit juices and flower nectar.

Thousands of gray-headed flying foxes gather in tree camps in Australia's eucalyptus forests and city parks.

The only megabats known to echolocate are Egyptian fruit bats. Instead of making sounds with their voice boxes, they click their tongues while flying through dark caves where they roost. Other megabats, though, roost out in the sunshine, hanging from top limbs of trees. Dozens may share a tree in colonies called camps, dangling like dark, hairy fruit.

Near sunset, megabats' toes let go of the branches as they fly off in search of an evening meal. All megabats are herbivores (HERB-uh-vorz), which are animals that eat plant material such as fruit, leaves, nectar, and pollen. The scent of night-blooming plants tempts nectar-loving species. A bat will hover before a bell-shaped flower and stick its nose inside. A long, bristled tongue slurps up the syrupy nectar, and pollen dusts the bat's fur. The bat will lick off some nutritious pollen, then deliver the rest to the next flower it visits. This pollen transfer, or pollination, allows the flower to produce seeds for the next generation of plants. While

Wahlberg's epauletted fruit bats fill their huge cheek pouches with ripe fruit. When they spit the seeds out later, they help the forest to grow new trees.

bees are resting at night, megabats are busy pollinating baobabs (BOW-babs), durian trees, and hundreds of other tropical plants.

Bananas, mangoes, dates, and other farmed and wild fruits also attract hungry megabats. Flat-topped back teeth, or molars, mash the soft fruit so a bat can swallow the juice and spit out much of the pulp and seeds. As it flies away, the seeds it spits out or leaves in its droppings can spread the plants to new places. Where trees have been cut down, those seeds can bring the rain forest back to life. Megabats' roles in spreading seeds and pollination are so important to tropical forests that scientists call them keystone species. These are animals that are key to the survival of a whole natural community.

Some microbats also eat fruit and nectar, including a few species living in the southern U.S. About 70% of all bat species, though, feed on insects. Many insects, like bats, are nocturnal (nok-TUR-nul), meaning that they are active by night and resting by day. Insectivore (in-SECT-uh-vore), or insect-eating, bats flit over meadows, through woods, and above backyards, gobbling bugs ranging from the tiniest gnats to saucer-sized moths. A little brown bat can stuff itself with several thousand moths, beetles, flies, and mosquitoes in one night. Microbats' huge appetites help protect wild plants and crops from insect damage, and protect humans from diseases carried by insects.

Among the many different kinds of microbats, some eat surprising types of food. Besides insects and plants, microbat diets may include spiders, mice, small birds, lizards, and even other bats. Frog-eating bats listen for mating calls of their prey and swoop down to pluck singing frogs off riverbanks. A fisherman bat skims over quiet ponds, echolocating to detect ripples in the water. Hearing the right signals, it drags hooked claws across the water's surface to snare the fish, then swoops up to a nearby perch. Sharp teeth crunch the bat's midnight lunch, bones and all.

When a fishing bat detects a minnow, it drags huge feet with sharp claws across the water. If this bat falls into the river, it can swim.

Three bat species in Central and South America may have the strangest diet of all: blood. Legends about vampires fill listeners with fear of blood-sucking monsters, but vampire bats are some of the most fascinating of all *Chiroptera*.

Extra-strong hind legs allow a vampire bat to land on the ground and run toward its prey, often a sleeping chicken, cow, or deer. Sharp front teeth cut a small slit in the victim's foot, where the bat laps up blood from the wound. Chemicals (KEM-ih-kuls) in the bat's saliva (sah-LI-vah) numb the cut so the animal stays asleep, and other

Bats
FUNFACT:

Less than 1/2 of 1% of bats catch rabies. Unlike dogs and cats, rabid bats rarely attack other animals. But never touch a bat you find because frightened animals can bite.

A vampire bat may spend a half hour lapping drips of blood from a small cut it makes in an animal's leg or tail.

chemicals, called anticoagulants (an-te-co-AG-u-lents), keep the blood flowing. After filling its stomach with about 1 tablespoon (15 ml) of blood, it returns to its roost. There, colony members squeal in hunger, and vampires cough up blood to feed the others.

Many people fear that vampire bats attack humans and, worse, carry a deadly disease called rabies (RAY-bees). In fact, any mammal can catch rabies, but the disease is quite rare. An ill bat can spread disease, but sick bats usually avoid humans.

Female Mexican free-tails arrive at Austin's Congress Avenue Bridge in March.
By August, their pups can also fly, so 1.5 million bats emerge each night.

Vampire colonies may include a few dozen members in a hollow tree or cave. Roosts of other species may shelter only one bat, perhaps a red bat dangling by one foot from a tree limb. And then there are some bat roosts, such as the Congress Avenue Bridge in Texas, which house over one million! Bats must find a safe place to rest each morning to avoid hawks and other daytime predators (PRED-uh-tors). Nocturnal hunters such as owls and snakes may still lurk by the roost entrance, waiting for the bats to emerge again at sundown.

In the tropics, bats roost in a variety of spots, such as inside animal burrows, termite nests, or flowers. Some roost in tents they make out of leaves. In North America, roosting bats can be found under loose tree bark, in caves and abandoned mines, in old barns, church steeples, and attics. Growing numbers even roost in boxes people build to attract bats.

Roosting bats are not just hanging around. Besides sleeping and quarreling with neighbors, they may climb the walls using their clawed thumbs to find a better roosting spot. Claws, tongue, and teeth also keep busy grooming the bat's fur. Although many see bats as dirty, they work hard to be as clean as cats. To stay clean, bats may even turn over and hang head up by their thumbs to release droppings.

A deep layer of droppings, called guano (GWAH-no), may pile up in caves used for decades by thousands of bats. Bat guano makes such rich, valuable fertilizer that people eagerly collect it no matter how much it stinks.

Some of the biggest roosts, such as Bracken Cave, shelter only female bats and their offspring, called pups. Each fall, male and female bats may court with wing displays, calls, and scent messages, but the pairs do not stay together after mating. Males fly to their own roosts and do not help raise the pups.

Scientists can measure the amount of guano in a cave to estimate how many bats live there.

Unlike other mammals, a female bat does not usually get pregnant right after mating. Instead, she stores the male's sperm in her body until spring. Only then is her egg fertilized. In a few weeks or months, depending on the species, a new bat will be born in a special roost called a nursery colony.

Bats living in the tropics may have pups twice a year, and a few kinds may have as many as four pups at a time. Most bats, though, have only one pup a year. When she is ready to deliver her baby, a female may turn over and hang by her thumbs. Her tail membrane and wings make a basket to catch the newborn. Once all the pups arrive in Bracken Cave, the colony's summer population soars from 20 million to 40 million bats!

Each newborn begins nursing right away, latching onto one of its mother's nipples with hooked milk teeth. Each mom licks and sniffs her baby, getting to know its unique smell and voice.

Eastern red bats are one of the few kinds that have two or more pups at a time.

Young fruit bats cling tightly to their mothers when they fly to find food at night, but many other baby bats stay behind in the roost. They cuddle together for warmth or, as they grow stronger, romp together like kittens on the cave ceiling. While the young rest and play, their mothers are hunting insects harder than ever, eating more than their body weight in bugs to make enough milk for their babies. When each female returns, she calls, sniffs, and listens until she finds her pup to nurse again.

Bats
FUNFACT:

Bats can purr! Like cats, a bat may vibrate, or purr, when resting and content.

Like many tropical bats, Gambian epauletted fruit bats may give birth twice a year.

Inside Bracken Cave, a mom returning from a hunt can identify
the sound and smell of her pup from millions of others.

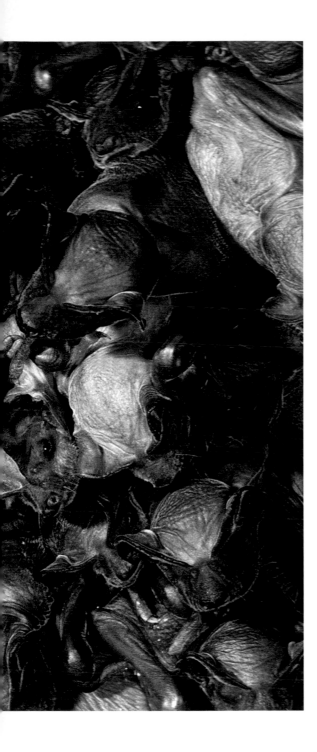

Bat pups grow fast. Mexican free-tails born in Bracken Cave arrive furless with eyes shut tight. Five hundred pink pups cram into each square foot (0.093 sq m) of cave wall! Soon the furry brown young can blink their eyes and stretch their wings, preparing for their first flight. At four or five weeks, they let go of the walls and drop into darkness. Meat-eating beetles scurry across the cave floor, waiting for any unlucky pups that fall. The rest practice flying in the cave until they are skilled enough to follow their mothers outside to hunt.

Lesser long-nosed bats are one of only three North American species that feed on fruit and night-blooming cacti and other nectar plants.

Bats living in the tropics can find insects, flowers, or other food year-round. In cooler climates, food supplies shrink each fall. Some bats, like many birds, travel to warmer places to spend the winter. When temperatures drop in the fall, hoary bats often head for Texas from summer homes as far north as Canada. Mexican free-tails in Bracken Cave and other U.S. roosts head even farther south, to Mexico and Central America. When spring returns, bats time their migration north to match the warming weather. Lesser long-nosed bats leave central Mexico when the agave (a-GAH-vee) begins to bloom and follow a path of cactus flowers 746 miles (1,200 km) to Arizona. These paths, or migratory corridors, are vital to the survival of the rare lesser long-nosed bat.

Bats
FUNFACT:

Hanging upside down for hours or even months is easy for bats. Their body weight locks their toes shut, so even dead bats keep hanging.

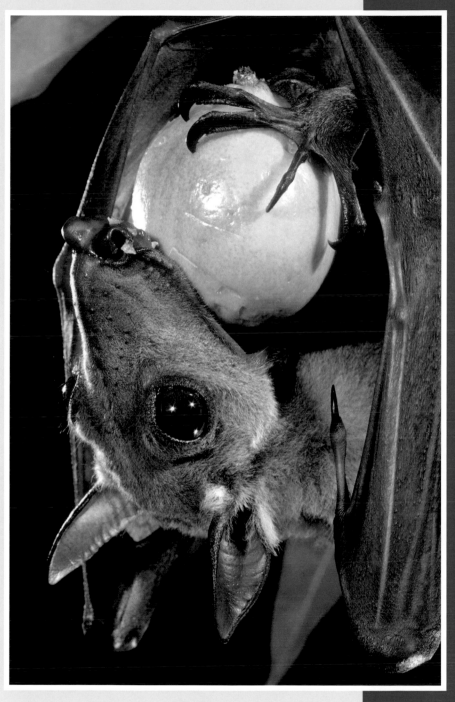

Hammer-headed fruit bats suck the juice of rose apples and other tropical fruits.

Nearly all gray bats hibernate in just eight caves in the southeastern U.S. With so few hibernacula, they are in danger of extinction.

Unlike birds, bats can also spend the winter in hibernation, a sleep-like state that saves energy when food is scarce. Little brown bats and most other U.S. and Canadian species feast on insects to store fat each fall. Then, in October, they seek safe winter roosts. Alone or in tight clusters, the bats fall into a deep sleep in which their temperature drops, their breathing slows, and their heart rate may fall from 400 to less than 25 beats per minute. This state is called torpor. Although they may wake a few times to stretch and sip water, bats may hibernate six months of the year.

Because they spend so much of their lives hibernating, bats must choose their winter shelters carefully. The ideal place, or hibernaculum (hi-ber-NAK-you-lum), should be safe from predators and warm enough to protect the bats from freezing all winter. A hibernaculum should also keep out human visitors, who might enter a cave or mine and disturb the bats. Waking from hibernation takes energy, and bats that awaken too often can use up their stored body fat and starve to death. Safe, warm places to hibernate are rare, so bats often return to the same spot, year after year.

Bats
FUNFACT:

Hubbard's Cave in Tennessee is one of the three most important caves for hibernating bats. A range of temperatures inside attracts seven different species, including endangered gray bats and Indiana bats. A metal grill keeps people from entering and disturbing the hibernators, but lets bats come and go.

Western pipistrelles are tiny bats also called canyon bats because they roost on cliffs and hunt for small insects in canyons in the western U.S.

Somehow, in their dark roosts, hibernating bats know when winter is ending. They look scruffy and thin after months without grooming or eating. But bats that survive their first winter have a good chance of living a long life.

Small mammals usually live only a few months or years, but most bats are not even grown up enough to reproduce until they are at least two years old. Bats may live 10 to 25 years in the wild, and one bat recently found in Siberia was at least 41 years old.

Bats face many dangers during their long lives. Predators, storms, and food shortages all kill bats. Some die when people wake them too often during hibernation or cut down trees where bats roost. Farmers shoot bats they blame for damaging fruit and accidentally poison bats with insecticides meant to keep bugs off crops. People who fear vampire bats blow up roosts sheltering whole colonies, and wind power generators kill growing numbers when bats crash into the propellers.

Because of all these threats, bats are disappearing around the world. Over half of the bat species in the U.S. and Canada are in trouble, and six species are in danger of dying out. Even many common species are seen less often every year.

People often fear vampire bats, but a protein from vampire saliva can help heal people after they have strokes.

Fortunately, bats also have many friends. Farmers who know bats eat tons of insect pests are using fewer insecticides, and other farmers are using nets instead of guns to keep bats off fruit trees. Cave explorers are helping to find bat colonies and put up special gates that let bats in but keep people out of roosts and hibernacula. Scientists are studying why bats crash into windmills to learn how to generate wind power safely. Conservation groups are working for bat protection laws and creating sanctuaries (SANK-choo-air-eez) to save migratory corridors, hibernacula, and other places bats need to survive.

Bats eat a wide variety of insects, including roaches and other bugs often viewed as pests.

Big brown bats often live close to people, roosting under bridges or inside old barns, church steeples, or specially made bat boxes.

Perhaps most important, educators are working to change attitudes toward bats. When people learn not to dread vampire bats, they leave the animals alone. Once people understand that bats are not dirty or diseased, they welcome bats in barns, under bridges, and in specially-built bat houses. Educators especially want people to learn that bats need open space. People need to protect the woods, caves, and other places where bats roost and hibernate as well as the meadows, forests, deserts, and other habitats where they feed. People who learn to care about bats can help them best by protecting their habitats.

Unlike other North American bats, spotted bats echolocate with low-pitched calls that humans can hear.

Bats may have to fly far from their roosts to find enough food each night. They need large areas where they can hunt safely.

You can help, too. Teach others the facts about bats. They are fascinating and valuable animals, important for eating insects that harm people and plants and for spreading pollen and seeds. Whether you watch them by night at Bracken Cave or in your own backyard, bats are a beautiful part of the natural world.

Internet Sites

You can find out more interesting information about bats and lots of other wildlife by visiting these Internet sites.

www.batcon.org   Bat Conservation International

www.enchantedlearning.com   Enchanted Learning

www.lubee.org   Lubee Bat Conservancy

www.nationalgeographic.com/kids/creature_feature/0110/vampirebats.html
                                                       National Geographic

http://batconservation.org   Organization for Bat Conservation

www.pbs.org/saf/1308/teaching/teaching.htm   Public Broadcasting Service

www.lhs.berkeley.edu/batquiz/   UC Berkeley Bat Quiz

www.ucmp.berkeley.edu/mammal/eutheria/chiroptera.html
                                                       University of California
                                                       Museum of Paleontology

Index

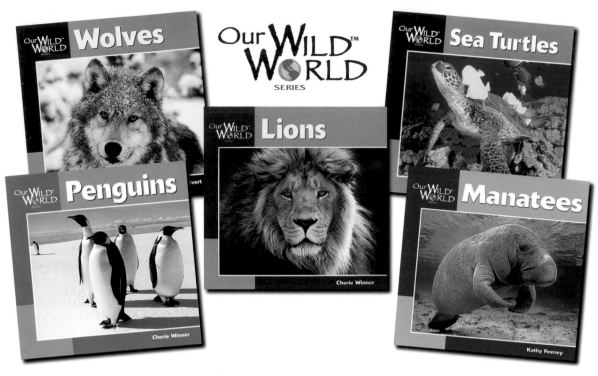

Titles available in the Our Wild World Series:

NorthWord
Minnetonka, Minnesota